Ducks

Ducks

DAVID JONES

Whitecap Books

Vancouver / Toronto

The information in this book is true and complete to the best of our knowledge. All
recommendations are made without guarantee on the part of the author or Whitecap
Books Ltd. The author and publisher disclaim any liability in connection with the use
of this information. For additional information please contact Whitecap Books Ltd.,
351 Lynn Avenue, North Vancouver, BC V7J 2C4. Information on this and other
Whitecap titles can also be found at the Whitecap web site: <www.whitecap.ca>.

Edited by Elizabeth McLean
Cover design by Steve Penner
Interior design by Margaret Ng
Desktop publishing by Tanya Lloyd

Printed in Canada.

Canadian Cataloguing in Publication Data

Jones, David (David Richard), 1956–
    Ducks

    Includes index.
    ISBN 1-55110-781-3

    1. Ducks. 2. Ducks—Pictorial works. I. Title.
QL696.A52J66 1998   598.4'1   C98-910654-3

The author is indebted to James R. Lovvorn, Associate Professor, Department of
Zoology, University of Wyoming, for his invaluable scientific advice.

There are rough drafts in nature; there are, in creation,
ready-made parodies; a bill which is not a bill,
wings which are not wings, fins which are not fins,
claws which are not claws, a mournful cry which
inspires us with the desire to laugh, there is the duck.

—Victor Hugo, *Les Misérables*

Standing barefoot on ice would be unbearable for us, but these mallards take it in stride. Experiments have shown that at temperatures down to the freezing point, ducks reduce the blood flow to their feet to prevent heat loss. At lower temperatures, however, the feet are in danger of damage due to freezing, and so blood flow increases again. The feet themselves do not require much blood, as most of the muscles controlling them are farther up the leg, well insulated by feathers.

C O N T E N T S

INTRODUCTION

THE UNLIKELY DUCK

A flock of blue-winged teal carves a turn in the air above an alpine lake and dips toward its dark surface. Splayed feet hiss across the water, and then the wings are tucked away, folded and gone. Here, on the mirror of air and water, the duck is at its most graceful: a feathered boat, seeming to move as effortlessly as a leaf on a river.

If only it would stay there, we might think of ducks as we think of swans. But the duck insists upon coming ashore, and the picture of grace heads south. We have our first good look at those cartoon feet. The Ojibwa have an explanation for them: Having lured the Chief of the ducks and his kind into a cave with the promise of music, the mythic hero Nanabozhoo throttled them one by one as they danced with their eyes closed. But one duck peeked and, seeing his dead brothers and sisters around him, bolted for the door. Nanabozhoo trod on the duck's feet as he fled, squashing them. Today, those flattened feet

PREVIOUS PAGE, RIGHT: *A male king eider struts across the ice. King eiders nest in a band circling the globe well north of the Arctic Circle, and even on its winter range, this bird seems to embrace some of the harshest climates on earth. Being the largest of all ducks is a great advantage under such conditions. Its greater size and round shape mean that the king eider has a proportionately reduced surface area, helping it to stay warm.*

PREVIOUS PAGE, LEFT: *The male common goldeneye, pictured here, can be distinguished from its closest relative, Barrow's goldeneye, by the shape of the cheek patches. In the common goldeneye, they're almost circular, white blobs. In Barrow's, they're teardrop shaped. The females of these two species are almost indistinguishable, but as hybrids are rare, it would seem that the drakes have no trouble telling them apart.*

impart a lurching, side-to-side motion to duck ambulation, a gait so awkward that a word had to be invented for it: waddle.

When the duck opens its bill, the last shreds of its dignity disappear. If Nana-bozhoo gave ducks their feet by stepping on them, he must have given them their voice when he wrung their necks. The mallard's strangled quack may be the reason animated cartoonists have consistently portrayed ducks as foul-tempered birds. Both Daffy and Donald are characterized by irritability and explosive fits of rage. Or perhaps the animators drew these characters after watching duck courtship, during which drakes try to woo Daisy mainly by attacking rival males. To the casual observer, it looks more like squabbling than foreplay.

LEFT: *Sea ducks taxi before becoming airborne because of their narrower wings, which are better suited to diving. Dabbling ducks, like this mallard, have broader wings that lift them almost vertically from the water's surface— a useful trick for a bird frequenting smaller bodies of water, where it is easier for predators to approach.*

Those of us living in cities tend to think of mallards when we think of ducks. Probably the most abundant of all waterfowl, the mallard has a remarkable tolerance for human beings and our cities; they are the ducks we are most likely to see in a ditch or backyard swimming pool. But mallards are just one of 35 species nesting in North America today, and of 125 species worldwide. One, the spectacled eider, has such a remote range that until 1995 no one even knew where they wintered.

Nor do we see ducks in great flocks in the city. Ask hunters or naturalists why they are drawn to ducks and they speak of their numbers. The air over a lake, churning with a thousand wings before the dawn, recalls a time on this continent that we can only imagine, of a land teeming with animal life.

According to Crow legend, ducks preceded even the continents, drifting on an ocean that covered the world. At that time, they were the sole animals. Old Man came to them one day, saying, "My brothers, there is earth below us. It is not good for us to be alone." He commanded four ducks to dive to the bottom of the ocean to retrieve mud. Only the bufflehead was successful, surfacing with a little mud on the webbing between its toes. Old Man spread the mud to form the continents, creating a home for all land animals and eventually the Crow people.

In evolutionary history, the duck holds a more modest place. Ducks recognizable to us as such probably appeared about 80 million years ago. Together with geese and swans, they form the family Anatidae—the scientific name for the world's 148 species of waterfowl.

It's natural to want to include the grebes, coots, and loons—birds that often share the

duck's habitat and lifestyle—with the waterfowl. Although these birds look like ducks, they are only distantly related to them. The waterfowl's closest living relatives are the flamingos and a group of South American birds known as screamers. Screamers resemble turkeys with enormous feet and bristly feathers around the head.

The delicate, hollow bones of birds are rarely fossilized, and so the early Anseriformes (screamers, flamingos, and waterfowl) have gone unrecorded in the fossil audit. Ornithologists bold enough to speculate on the form of the duck ancestor envision a bird that looked something like a flamingo, but with a shorter neck and legs. It lived at the margins of shallow, tropical lakes similar to those in Africa's Great Rift Valley today and fed by straining algae or other plankton from the mud, much as modern flamingos do.

The offspring of some of these birds came to spend more time swimming and less wading (flamingos are actually quite good swimmers), as they dabbled for their food. Over eons, their descendants developed shorter legs and flared bills resembling a modern duck's. From this ancestral waterfowl arose the modern Anatidae.

Ducks differ from geese and swans in several ways: They mature more rapidly—usually within a single season—and only a few species grow as large as even a small goose. They molt twice a year. While many geese and swans mate for life, male ducks depart shortly after the hen begins laying. In all but a few species, their plumage is strikingly different from the females'.

Although small as waterfowl go, ducks are large birds. The biggest North American duck, the common eider, can weigh as much as 2.7 kilograms (6 pounds). Their powerful flight muscles offer an ample supply of meat, rich in fat. For predators in cold climates, this

LEFT: *In addition to diving for fish, the red-breasted merganser will often swim with only its head submerged as a kind of reverse periscope, searching for prey. Occasionally, these ducks coordinate hunting efforts, moving in a line to corral fish into shore before snapping them up.*

PREVIOUS PAGE: *The ugly duckling of the Hans Christian Andersen fable turns out not to be a duck at all, but a swan mistakenly raised by ducks. Persecuted by its siblings and the other animals, the swan flees the cruelty of the barnyard to spend winter in a marsh, where it is saved from death by a group of kind swans.*

package of calories is irresistible. Moreover, ducks molt, migrate and winter in flocks, raising the prospect of multiple kills.

Primitive hunters must have viewed their first flock of ducks as manna, and the ducks have been giving ever since. Before acquiring firearms, the Inuit used bolas made of ivory or whale bone to bring down ducks crossing headlands in foggy weather. They sometimes ensnared up to three birds with a single throw when a flock emerged from the mist.

The Quinault tribe of the Olympic Peninsula in Washington State stretched nettle fiber nets about 6 metres (20 feet) square across streams where they had seen canvasbacks or teal flying. The nets were suspended about 5 metres (16 feet) above the watercourse, usually between two trees. Nettle fibers can be woven finely enough that the ducks would see the nets too late to avoid entanglement, particularly at dusk. The Salish to the north used a similar technique, but preferred to hang their nets between poles, sometimes reaching 12 metres (40 feet) into the air.

Farther south, the Aztecs used the pole-and-net technique to capture waterfowl on the margins of Lake Texcoco, but they were also skilled in the use of blowpipes and darts. Montezuma is reported to have made a gift of 20 golden ducks and a jewel-encrusted blow-pipe to Cortés.

The duck's habit of sleeping on the water, close to shore, made it easy for native peoples to hunt them at night, sometimes dazzling the birds with the light of torches before clubbing them with poles or pelting them with stones. Ducks drifting into the shallows during their molts were even easier prey.

The Skagit tribe of western Washington State preferred a more subtle technique,

employing painted ducks carved from blocks of cedar. A swimmer would drag the decoys to the bottom of the lake, where spirits would animate them. Once they had bobbed back to the surface, these cedar ducks possessed many powers, among them the ability to guard property and call living ducks down from the sky.

Modern duck hunters are equally familiar with the magic of wood carved and painted in the form of a duck. Since the invention of firearms, they have used calls and floating decoys to entice flocks to light within range of a blind or other concealment. Over time, decoy carving and duck calling have developed into art forms of their own.

The word decoy is actually derived from the old Dutch words *de kooi,* meaning "the cage." Originally, the word referred to mazes of mesh or netting into which European hunters would lure inquisitive ducks—sometimes with a small tolling dog, sometimes with carved decoys in the modern sense of the word—to slaughter the birds, or pinion them for captivity.

Its flesh is not the duck's only gift to humans. Most peoples who have hunted ducks also raided their large clutches of eggs. The nests of many duck species yield a special dividend: the fluffy, inner down feathers which the hen plucks from her breast to cushion and insulate her eggs.

Eiders nest in colonies numbering in the thousands and when brooding is completed, the hens abandon the shallow bowls of down to the wind. Even today, dry down is a more effective insulator than the best synthetics. To make their warmest parkas, the Inuit sewed together dozens of eider skins in two layers, the feathers sandwiching a perfect, insulating air space.

LEFT: *The ruddy duck is a member of the stifftail tribe, which feeds by diving to the bottoms of lakes or ponds and then sifting through the sediment, much in the manner of a surface-feeding dabbler. In addition to using its rudder-like tail to steer underwater, the male ruddy duck also cocks it forward as part of some courtship displays.*

PREVIOUS PAGE: *The northern pintail was once the most numerous duck in North America after the mallard, thanks in part to its adaptability. Pintails eat whatever food they find in abundance, mainly dabbling, but also feeding on grains and other land plants. No one is sure why their numbers have declined so severely over the last 15 years.*

The flight and head feathers of the mallard and wood duck are among the most colorful of any bird's in North America, and native peoples from the Haida to the Aztecs sought them for mantles, ceremonial blankets, and headdresses. The Hopi prized mallard feathers above any other bird's except the eagle. To the Hopi, ducks are the couriers of souls and messages to the next world—a belief inspired, perhaps, by the directness of their migratory flights and the urgency of their wingbeats. In flight, ducks always appear to be hurrying.

Perhaps no people held the duck in higher esteem than the ancient Aztecs. Ehecatl is the Aztec god of the wind, and one of the most powerful figures in Aztec mythology. Carvings and statuary depict Ehecatl in his human form wearing a buccal mask—a beak or a muzzle strapped over the mouth. The mask strongly resembles a duck's bill. Why ducks, above all other birds, should be the incarnation of winds and storms is not known. As hurricanes cause as much of their destruction through waves as the wind itself, the duck—equally at home in air and water—may have seemed an appropriate avatar.

The Aztecs found no contradiction in eating the animals they deified. They saw game as a gift of nature. So did some of the first European visitors to North America, who found flocks of ducks so curious that they could be attracted by almost any commotion—clapping, whistling, or yelling. As recently as 1925, the naturalist and hunter John Phillips wrote of the ruddy duck, "Indeed, it would be hard to imagine a tamer duck, and one that has profited less by the noisy education delivered to it so regularly by the shooting public."

Perhaps that is what endears the duck to us. Despite centuries of education at the sharp end of human invention, its curiosity and its abundance still make it a gift to hunters, naturalists, and the children who throw bread to it in the park.

LEFT: *According to Crow legend, the first animals were ducks. Asked by Old Man to bring forth mud from the bottom of the great ocean, only the bufflehead succeeded. The mud he carried on the webbing between his toes became the continents, home to animals and humans alike.*

ABOVE: *Ducks taking flight may signal one another with displays of chin wagging or neck stretching to cue the moment of take-off. Simultaneous takeoff is important because of the protection it offers against predators, who often catch stragglers.*

RIGHT: *A small duck, such as this green-winged teal, may have as few as 11 500 feathers, while a big eider may have over twice that many. Surprisingly, the majority of the feathers on a duck's body are the tiny ones covering its head and neck— the one area that it can't preen with its bill. It can, however, scratch its head with its foot.*

RIGHT: *The scientific name for the wood duck,* Aix sponsa, *translates as "waterfowl in bridal dress." This is probably a reference to the male's nuptial plumage, which is far more spectacular than the female's comparatively drab colors.*

ABOVE: *The American wigeon has a reputation for being something of a scrounger. Though a dabbling duck, it has a taste for bottom plants such as wild celery. To get these foods, it often waits for superior divers such as red-heads or coots to surface, so it can poach some of their catch.*

ABOVE: *Oldsquaws nest on the tundra, where groundcover is sparse and they must rely upon their plumage to camouflage their nests. This female has flattened herself over her eggs in an effort to hide them. Even when she leaves the nest to bathe or to feed, down plucked from her breast and spread over the eggs will continue to protect her clutch by keeping it warm and hidden.*

RIGHT: *The gadwall seems a thoroughly modest duck. Its plumage is a conservative pattern of browns, blacks, and grays, with its showiest marking a pair of white wing flashes that it displays only in flight. Consistent with its retiring image, the gadwall's nest is usually hidden in dense groundcover. It may also nest on islands, which provide added security from predators.*

RIGHT: *Clean, turbulent water is vital habitat for harlequins. They spend their summers hunting for insect larvae in the pools and rapids of mountain streams and nest along their banks—either under brush or in a tree cavity. In winter, they hunt for invertebrates along surf-pounded shores. The scarcity of such pristine habitat has taken its toll on harlequins, which have been an endangered species for about a decade.*

DABBLERS AND DIVERS

LIFE ON AND UNDER WATER

The Arctic Ocean is a long way from a bread-strewn pond in the park, but there are ducks there, 50 metres (165 feet) deep, foraging in the near darkness for shellfish and crustaceans. The oldsquaw propels itself to these depths with webbed feet set far back on its body—a characteristic of the diving ducks. Occasionally, it supplements its paddling with a flap of its wings. Reaching the bottom is not easy, even for these strong swimmers. That's because ducks rely on a layer of down and air, trapped beneath their feathers, to keep warm. In effect, they are swimming inside a bubble, and it's far lighter than the blubber that insulates diving mammals. This natural life jacket is most buoyant in the first few metres of the duck's descent, before water pressure compresses it. Not until the oldsquaw passes a depth of some 45 metres (140 feet) is it able to stay down without effort.

PREVIOUS PAGE, LEFT: *The bill of the merganser is like a pair of pliers, perfect for catching small fish. While most fish-eating ducks surprise their prey by snatching them from above, the mergansers are such fast underwater swimmers that they can actually chase down fish. The red-breasted merganser, pictured here, rarely leaves salt water except during breeding season.*

PREVIOUS PAGE, RIGHT: *When not feeding or sleeping, ducks spend much of their time preening. Part of this ritual involves combing or plucking out damaged feathers. With their flexible necks, ducks can reach almost every feather on their body below the neck—as this northern pintail is demonstrating.*

Once on the bottom, the oldsquaw tears mussels or other bivalves from the rocks with its blunt and powerful bill. It may crack the mussel's shell or swallow it whole, underwater, allowing its gizzard to do the work. The gizzards of sea ducks are so strong that it's possible to hear the grinding of shells inside the duck.

Oldsquaws are among the most specialized of the diving ducks, which is one of the two broad types of duck. While all ducks feed on and around water, diving ducks regularly forage by submerging their whole bodies. Divers include the goldeneyes, canvasback, scoters, eiders, and mergansers. The sea ducks eat mainly fish and shellfish. Some freshwater diving ducks fish, but many, like the canvasback, grub in the sediment for aquatic tubers.

The other kind of duck is the dabblers. Dabbling ducks feed by dipping their

LEFT: *Oldsquaws are capable of diving to greater depths than any other duck—at least 60 metres (200 feet). Because of their deep-diving abilities, they often float in rafts far offshore where they are safe from most predators yet still able to reach the bottom to forage for their chief foods—marine invertebrates. Their curious name comes from their yodel-like call, which inexplicably reminded early American naturalists of women's voices.*

spatulate bills into the water or mud. They also forage in shallow water by "tipping up"—reaching to the pond bottom with their bills while their feet and tail feathers wave in the air. Mallards are dabbling ducks, as are the shovelers, teals, pintails, wigeons, gadwall, and the American black duck.

The ducks are not particularly mindful of these categories, however. Dabblers may dive and divers may dabble. To further complicate matters, biologists recognize nine duck tribes, all but two of which are represented in North America. The four dabbling tribes are the shelduck tribe, the perching duck tribe, the whistling duck tribe, and the dabbling tribe (not to be confused with the general category of dabbling duck).

The three diving duck tribes represented in North America are the seaduck, pochard, and stifftail tribes. Some of these names are rather misleading. Seaducks such as the harlequin and the surf scoter nest in forests many miles inland and will dive in fresh water.

The divers share a number of adaptations to hunting below the surface. Their feet are set well back on their bodies so that they can push from the rear. Their wings are generally not as broad as those of the dabblers, making them less buoyant. Some diving ducks flap their wings underwater to assist propulsion with their feet.

There are costs to these adaptations. The legs of some divers are positioned so far back that they can barely walk, leaving them more vulnerable to predators when they must come ashore to nest. Smaller wings provide less lift than broad ones, which can make for long takeoffs. The red-breasted merganser cannot take flight without first taxiing over the water for several seconds to get up to speed. By comparison, the larger wings of a dabbling duck such as the mallard can have it airborne in a single beat.

All birds have internal air sacs connected directly to the lungs, but in diving ducks these sacs are considerably smaller, reducing the duck's buoyancy. Some biologists speculate that on long dives the air in these sacs may be stirred and exchanged with air in the lungs by the muscular action of swimming, in effect giving the diving duck the benefit of a larger lung capacity. When a duck's face enters the water, its heart rate immediately drops by about two-thirds—especially if the duck is forced underwater or frightened into diving. On long dives, blood flow is diverted from the other organs to the heart and brain to conserve oxygen.

Dabblers are distinguished by their own set of physiological adaptations—in particular, their marvelous bills. When we hear the term duck bill, most of us picture the spatulate bill of the dabblers. It's such a successful feeding tool that no fewer than three classes of animal have employed it—the birds, the reptiles (in the extinct hadrosaurs), and, in at least one instance, the mammals (the platypus).

The flared bill makes a good shovel to root through mud and is useful for tearing off parts of aquatic plants that would shred into bits in the grip of a narrower beak. It also works as a catcher's mitt to snatch invertebrates or vegetable matter from the water.

But how does a duck manipulate such tiny food with a rigid bill? The bills of dabbling ducks are serrated with tiny ridges called lamellae that run perpendicular to the rim. The duck takes water or mud in through its open bill, then closes it and forces the water out through the sides. Food particles are trapped by the lamellae, which the duck then licks off with its tongue, and swallows. This sieving technique is most highly developed in the northern shoveler, which has such closely spaced lamellae that it can strain organisms as small as diatoms from the water. There may be as many as a thousand different species of diatoms. Of those,

only a few giants exceed half the size of a period on this page. And yet this duck feeds so efficiently that such microscopic organisms are a mainstay of its diet.

In the diving ducks, the counterpart to the dabbler's lamellae are the serrations of the merganser's saw-toothed bill. They use these bills to grasp and manipulate the small fish and large aquatic insects which are their main prey. Fast underwater swimmers, the mergansers chase and catch fish during their dives. Once back on the surface, they may have to struggle for several minutes with larger fish before swallowing them, so a good grip is essential.

Stifftail ducks, such as the ruddy duck and the masked duck, employ a combination diving/dabbling feeding technique. They submerge completely like other diving ducks, then sift through the mud at the bottom with a spatulate bill in the manner of a dabbler.

LEFT: *The northern shoveler's huge bill is a superbly adapted organ for sieving through mud or water for microscopic plants and animals, which make up a considerable portion of its diet. Shovelers are so good at gleaning food in this way that they may feed for up to an hour without moving more than a body length from their original position.*

Ducks don't always feed in the water. The American wigeon has a small bill adapted to grazing on grasses, much like that of a goose. Wood ducks search the forest floors for nuts, seeds, and berries dropped from trees. In shallows overhung by oaks, they often tip-up, scouring the bottom for acorns, fallen fruit, and the more usual duck foods such as duckweed and wild celery. They will even make a meal of a frog or salamander if they catch one.

Whatever its diet, a duck's bill serves another function almost as vital as feeding. Preening is not an act of vanity in birds; it's vital to their health, and the bill is the duck's main preening tool. With up to 20 000 feathers covering a large duck's body, grooming is a big job.

Ducks often begin a preening session with a bath. The idea of an animal that spends most of its time in water taking a bath may seem a little odd, but a bathing duck splashes its wings and head in a very deliberate way to wash dirt and debris from under the flight feathers. Then it shakes its body and wings to shed excess water. The duck pulls mussed or bent flight feathers through its bill, using the lamellae like the teeth of a comb to align the barbs. It may nibble feathers to weave their barbs into a continuous, interlocking cover. Feathers too damaged to be properly aligned are plucked out. The duck's flexible neck allows it to reach almost every part of its body below the collar. Apart from those ducks with crests, the head feathers tend to be much shorter than the plumage covering the rest of the body and, like a crew cut, don't require much maintenance anyway.

LEFT: *In keeping with the eccentric nature of duck nomenclature, the wood duck—graced with some of the most spectacular markings of all North American birds—is named for its habitat. The wood duck nests in trees, and was christened by early naturalists who saw it searching wooded areas for the tree cavities in which the female lays her eggs.*

Finally, the duck rubs its feathers with oil, which it spreads from the uropygial glands at the base of its tail. Again, the bill is its main tool. The duck rubs the bill on the glands to stimulate them, then smears the oiled bill over its feathers.

Plumage maintained in this way is completely waterproof and keeps waterfowl warm in the coldest of weather. Some eider populations around Hudson Bay migrate only if forced by complete closure of the sea ice. They may endure temperatures as low as −45° Celsius (−50° Fahrenheit) and feed in water a few degrees below freezing.

Harlequins are divers with especially smooth, compact feathers that trap even more air than the plumage of other ducks—probably to protect their smaller bodies from the cold. The water in which they dive isn't as cold as that inhabited by the eiders, but it poses its own dangers. In summer, harlequins shoot the rapids and pools of remote mountain streams, diving for the larvae of caddis flies and other insects. In the winter, they forage for mussels and other invertebrates between waves slamming rocky shorelines. It may seem an unnecessary risk, but these churning waters—marine and fresh—are well oxygenated and support an abundance of life. The harlequins sometimes pay the price with broken bones, but usually heal to hunt another day.

The only parts of the body that duck feathers cannot protect from the cold are the bill and feet. The feet are particularly problematic. Being large and flat, they are natural radiators and would lose a lot of heat to the environment were it not for a system of heat exchangers in the duck's legs. The arteries supplying blood to the feet pass alongside the veins removing blood. The warm arterial blood is cooled by the venous blood before entering the feet, and the cooler venous blood is warmed as it enters the body. In this way, very little of the duck's

LEFT: *Male surf scoters are easily identified by their colorful bills. As with most ducks, the female is drab by comparison, but her bill shares the same peculiar form. Its oddly warped shape looks a bit like a classic duck bill that was left too near the stove. It is nonetheless effective for plucking mollusks, crabs, and other invertebrates from the sea bottom and crushing their shells. This scoter has found a mussel.*

body heat ever reaches its feet. Like most birds, the duck can also draw its feet up into its flank feathers when flying or sitting to keep them warm.

Similarly, ducks protect their bills in cold weather by tucking their heads under their wings. But in hot weather, the bill is an important heat regulator, radiating heat to the air and water. The bill is also the site of the outlet of the salt excretion glands, which allow the seaducks to drink salt water when fresh water isn't available.

The duck has evolved a remarkable series of behavioral and physiological adaptations. There are birds that are more skilled fliers; penguins and marine mammals dive deeper—but there is no animal as adept at both flying and swimming as the duck.

The one thing it does not do well is walk, but as the expression goes, one does not fault a bear for dancing badly; rather, one marvels that it can dance at all.

LEFT: *Even with their characteristic green heads submerged, these ducks are clearly identifiable as male mallards by the cowlick of the tail coverts. (Coverts are small feathers that cover the bases of large ones.) As one astute observer of waterfowl put it, "Ducks have cute underwear."*

RIGHT: *The lesser scaup, pictured here, is distinguished from its nearest relative, the greater scaup, by the color of the male's head. Greater scaups have a greenish sheen to their head feathers, while the head of the lesser scaup is more purplish. The lesser scaup is more likely to be found on freshwater than its cousin.*

ABOVE: *An American wigeon at takeoff flashes its white wing patches. This duck's white forehead and scalp give it its other popular name of baldpate. Many ducks hold their webbed feet edge-on in the direction of flight, reducing drag until they fold them against their bodies.*

ABOVE: *The northern pintail is widely distributed, nesting over an enormous range circling the northern hemisphere. Some pintails undertake extremely difficult migrations—one population winters in Hawaii and breeds in Alaska.*

RIGHT: *The apparent shape of the hooded merganser's head varies dramatically with its mood. In this shot, the crest is erect, giving this male the appearance of having a very large head. The hooded merganser's rather small body size emphasizes this impression. In flight, with the crest feathers folded, the head looks about half this size.*

DUCKS AND DRAKES

RITES OF REPRODUCTION

The dances of ducks are manifold: Steaming. Bridling. Bubbling. The Burp. Different species may perform the same dances, but never in the same way, or in the same order. These rituals may seem a waste of energy, but they serve a special purpose: In effect, they are secret handshakes. Knowing the moves, which are acts of pure instinct, is a sign of membership in the most exclusive club of all, the club of species.

Combined with the male's distinctive plumage, the dances—properly called displays—allow ducks to form and reinforce the pair bond necessary for the female to submit to mating. By watching competing males display, females choose a mate that is healthy, attentive, and aggressive—characteristics that will be of great help to her in the coming weeks. The display also assures that, even when different species court on the same grounds, females select males of their own kind.

PREVIOUS PAGE, LEFT: *One of the ironies of duck life is that in order to remain dry, they have to bathe. This wood duck is not bathing out of vanity, but to retain his feathers' properties of water repellence by cleaning them thoroughly. He will follow his bath with preening to re-oil the feathers.*

PREVIOUS PAGE, RIGHT: *The common goldeneye has a bewildering repertoire of courtship displays. The male in this photo signals his interest in a nearby female with the head-throw display, which is usually accompanied by a rattling call.*

If it were not for the rituals of courtship display, some species physically capable of producing hybrids might interbreed. This may be precisely what is happening to the American black duck, a dabbling duck that is now interbreeding with the mallard in large numbers. Before this century, mallards were rare in the eastern half of the United States, the black duck's primary range. But breeding programs to supply hunters with game introduced hundreds of thousands of mallards into Pennsylvania and Maryland. The courtship displays of the two species are quite similar, and the more aggressive mallard males began successfully courting black duck females, with the result that genetically pure American black ducks have declined.

LEFT: *Ducks have a wide variety of calls, and usually male and female vocalizations are entirely different. As with other waterfowl, male ducks of many species have a bony sound chamber at the base of the trachea called the bulla, which affects the sound of the male's call. In ducks without a bulla, the sound usually emanates from tympanic membranes between the base of the windpipe and the bronchial tubes. This American wigeon's call is a thin, breathy whistle.*

In addition to ensuring species fidelity, courtship displays reinforce the pair bond and bring the couple into mating readiness at about the same time.

Ruddy ducks bubble—a display in which one male threatens another by cocking his tail and drumming special air sacs in his neck and upper chest with his bill. At the same time, air trapped beneath the breast feathers is forced into the water, and so the name bubbling. Bubbling often ends with the burp—a sudden expulsion of air from the tracheal sacs.

In ritualized drinking, courting mergansers drink to one another by dipping their bills in the water and then raising them, as if upending a glass.

There are dozens of these displays, but many biologists, including legendary animal behaviorist Konrad Lorenz, believe that one display above all others typifies the ducks. Exclusive to females, it's called the inciting display. With a specific sequence of movements, she "incites" a potential mate to attack or chase a third duck—male or female. The prospective mate's fitness is evaluated by his response. The more effective his defence of the female, the more appealing she finds him.

In its purest form, exhibited by some of the shelducks, the inciting display has two parts: In the first, the hen signals in the direction of the preferred male. Chin-lifting is a typical motion. In the second, she indicates the male to be driven off by, for example, bowing low and pointing her head at him. The two parts may be alternated repeatedly, and either motion may be accompanied by a call of some kind.

In most duck species, inciting displays are not so pointed. Hens may simply repeat a motion such as chin-lifting, accompanied by a particular call. Depending on his enthusiasm,

the male may attack any nearby male, or he may choose a less aggressive response, such as head-pumping (reminiscent of a strutting pigeon). The drake may further respond to the female with a ritual display of preening-behind-the-wing. Many courtship displays are practical behaviors that have been highly stylized: Drinking, preening, and bathing motions are all represented in displays.

These courtship displays may begin long before the pair actually reaches the spring nesting grounds, on the lakes, ponds, and estuaries where the ducks winter. Wood ducks, pintails, mallards, and eiders often pair off as early as the fall.

Ducks exhibit nonsexual displays, too. Neck-jerking or head-shaking constitute an agreement among flock members that they are all about to take off. If you've ever wondered how a flock of ducks can spring from the surface of a lake or pond as one, it's because they've signalled to each other beforehand, the equivalent of saying, "One, two, three, go!"

Migrating birds begin their flight to the breeding grounds in late winter or early spring. This may be a hop across the pond in the case of a mallard in southern California, which may not migrate at all, or a journey of 11 300 kilometres (7000 miles) in the case of a blue-winged teal migrating from Peru to the Athabasca River delta in northern Alberta. A harlequin duck wintering on the British Columbia coast may fly inland a stone's throw or across whole mountain ranges to reach the banks of the rushing forest stream where it will lay its eggs.

The ultimate destination comes as a surprise to the paired drake as he follows his chosen mate back to her nesting ground of the previous year. Because ducks choose new mates annually, a drake that mated in Texas one spring may find himself in the potholes of Saskatchewan the next.

LEFT: *The harlequin's common name refers to its markings, which are so sharply delineated they resemble the costume of a harlequin—the masked clown who played the medieval stage. In particular, the duck's head crest looks like the clown's bicorn hat. Even the harlequin's scientific name,* Histrionicus histrionicus, *refers to acting and drama.*

PREVIOUS PAGE: *Preening-behind-the-wing is a common display among ducks. Males use it to indicate their interest in females, and females may signal their approval of a male's attack on a rival with this display. When a duck simply preens behind the wing to groom its feathers, the action is much less deliberate.*

As a rule, ducks migrate in flocks but occasionally they will travel as an isolated pair. When the birds stop to rest on ponds or lakes along the way, the pair bond is further strengthened by synchronized preening. Copulation may take place during the migration, or once the birds have arrived at their destination. Sometimes a pair bond that held during migration is broken by aggressive single males on the nesting grounds.

Ducks mate on the water. Typically, after signalling each other with a display such as mutual head-pumping, the hen indicates her willingness to copulate by stretching her neck low over the water. The drake mounts her from behind, sometimes sinking her right up to the

FAR LEFT: *The female common goldeneye indicates her willingness to mate by flattening herself on the water so that her eyes are just clear of the surface. The male, nearby, performs the masthead display.*

LEFT: *Finally, the male mounts her, securing his position by gripping the female's head feathers with his bill. After copulation, the male may circle the female several times while still gripping her head.*

bill, which she must hold above water like a snorkel. Drakes have been known to drown females by holding them under for too long. This is most likely to happen during a rape, which some males may resort to late in the breeding season if they haven't paired. Such frustrated males are common because in most duck species, they outnumber females. Females suffer higher mortality rates than males while nesting and rearing, when they are more vulnerable to predators.

Usually, the female keeps her head above water by "treading" for anywhere from 10 seconds to a few minutes. Most birds and reptiles achieve fertilization by pressing the vents of their cloacae together. The cloaca is a bodily chamber into which both waste products and sperm or eggs are emptied and held before leaving the body. Male ducks, however, have a corkscrew-shaped penis that has probably evolved to help the drake stay in place during treading, as it penetrates the female's cloaca. The male often reinforces his mount by grasping the feathers at the nape of the female's neck with his bill.

Staying in place is particularly difficult for harlequins, which may be copulating in the rapids of a mountain stream. Sometimes the pair will be swept underwater and bob to the surface again well downstream from their starting point.

After mating, there are more displays. The male often faces the female and watches her preen behind the wings. Male scaups and mergansers steam—a ritual in which they turn their backs on the female and retreat a short distance. Other ducks bridle, rearing their heads in a motion a little like a bridling horse. Females of many species complete their coupling rituals with a bath, and males often join in.

Duck nests are not the elaborate structures built by songbirds. For most ground-nesting

ducks, a natural depression in the soil or weeds is about all the inspiration that the female needs to begin laying, and it is not until later that she adds nesting materials. Most of the dabbling ducks prefer an area with tall grass or shrubs to conceal their clutches, but others may nest in shorter vegetation, relying entirely on their drab plumages for camouflage. Curiously, waterfowl are incapable of carrying objects any distance as other birds do. They can drag grasses or leaves toward themselves, but they can't walk and carry at the same time. Thus, their nesting materials are restricted to objects within reach, including their own down feathers. These, they pluck from their breasts to use as a covering for the eggs in their absence.

Ground-nesters prefer a location adjacent to the water in tall grass, but will nest up to a kilometre and a half (one mile) away. Some construct nests on floating mats of grasses or reeds, creating a kind of nesting island. The fulvous whistling duck may conceal her nest with a dome of grasses or sedges.

Many of the diving ducks build floating nests, which discourage predators that avoid water, such as foxes.

Other species, including buffleheads, goldeneyes, mergansers, and wood ducks, nest in tree cavities. For these birds, the only nesting materials within reach are their feathers, which they use to line the cavity. A nest in a tree hole offers more protection than a loose circle of grass. Even if a predator finds a cavity nest, the mother may be able to defend it against an intruder whose only access is through a small hole.

But vacant tree cavities are not easy to come by. They generally occur in old, dead

LEFT: *Scaups are probably named for the male's call, which sounds like the word* scaup *uttered twice. A competing theory holds that the name is a corruption of scalp, an obsolete term for mussel beds. Mussels make up a good part of the diet of the greater scaup, pictured here.*

trees, which are becoming increasingly scarce as old-growth forests dwindle. Those that are left are in high demand by squirrels, bees, bats, flickers, and dozens of other animals.

Lighting precisely on the rim of a nest hole would seem to be something of a feat for a heavy bird like a duck. The wood duck has larger eyes, broader wings, and a longer tail than most ducks to help it maneuver through woods at lower flight speeds. But the diving ducks, with their comparatively small wings, seem to manage just as well.

Regardless of the nest type, it is the hen that selects the site, although the male will often accompany her on her search. The drakes of most species will stay until the laying of the last eggs and leave sometime after incubation has begun, but they never assist in this task. Nor do they bring the hen any food.

Most males abandon the female shortly after incubation begins. Many of them will seek another mate—willing or not—so they can father a second brood. One of the few drakes to stay with his mate is the fulvous whistling duck, which lingers near the nest to assist with rearing. His rather drab nuptial plumage is almost indistinguishable from the female's, supporting the theory that one of the reasons most male ducks don't help with incubation is to avoid attracting predators to the nest.

If the father plays so little part in nesting and rearing, why should ducks go to such lengths to establish pair bonds? It seems that the male's second most important contribution to reproduction may occur well before copulation. Studies of eiders and other ducks have shown that a paired female has much more time to dabble or hunt than an unpaired female during the crucial months before nesting. During this time, her mate drives off potential suitors who would otherwise harass the female. This leaves her free to feed and build the fat reserves

LEFT: *This oldsquaw nest was probably abandoned by a frightened or disturbed hen. When a female leaves a nest temporarily to feed, she always covers the eggs with some of the surrounding down, to keep them warm and hidden. Ducks are ill equipped to defend against most other animals, but they have a few tricks. On approach of a predator, the female hops away from the nest trailing an open wing in an effort to draw the intruder's attention away from her clutch.*

essential for the nesting period to come. In this way, the male duck may provide for his offspring before they are even conceived.

Similarly, some male ducks establish a territory within a short flight of their mate's nest. During egg laying and the first days of incubation, they wait for the female at this appointed location, and chase away all other suitors and interloping pairs. Once or twice a day she flies there to feed and preen where her alert and aggressive mate can protect her from the advances of other males.

Gradually, however, the pair bond deteriorates, and drakes begin to congregate with other males. Eventually, the males fly off to molting areas, where they trade their colorful nuptial feathers for the rather more drab eclipse plumage. Most eclipse plumages leave the males looking very much like the females of their species for about a month. This plumage provides better camouflage than their nuptial feathers, which they won't be needing for a few months anyway. Remaining inconspicuous is especially important during the weeks before their flight feathers grow in again. Unable to fly, they tend to remain out of sight in tall aquatic vegetation or linger far offshore on larger lakes.

Back at the nest, the female is incubating her eggs. Ducks lay very large clutches. Most species lay an average of 9 or 10 pale green, white, or beige eggs one at a time, usually in the early morning. The hen begins laying her eggs within a day of copulation, but doesn't start incubation until all the eggs are laid to ensure that the young will hatch simultaneously. If they did not all hatch at once, the female would be left the impossible task of shepherding around one group of ducklings while incubating the remainder still in their shells.

RIGHT: *The redhead is known for the large numbers of eggs it lays—often in other ducks' nests. This habit allows the redhead to avoid keeping all her eggs in one basket—a viable strategy, considering the high percentage of duck nests destroyed by predators.*

PREVIOUS PAGE: *A white eye ring and grayish head distinguish these black-bellied whistling ducks from the fulvous whistling duck. Named for their whistle-like calls in flight, whistling ducks walk upright, similarly to geese. The sexes are hard to tell apart, and males help to build the nest, incubate the eggs and rear the ducklings.*

Rather than incubating their own eggs, some hens find an unattended nest and lay their eggs in it. Redheads parasitize other nests to varying degrees. Some lay a normal clutch of about nine eggs, which they incubate, then lay additional eggs in a neighbor's nest—a behavior known as dumping. Other redheads don't incubate any of their own eggs, dumping them all.

If several females dump into the same nest, a clutch may become absurdly large, as in the case of the single redhead nest containing 87 eggs. Redheads will also parasitize the nests of other species—primarily canvasbacks. Fulvous whistling duck nests holding as many as 100 eggs have been found and are clearly the result of dumping.

Dumped eggs have a rather poor survival rate. Often, there are too many eggs for the adoptive mother to cover completely. If incubation of the host's eggs is well underway at the time of the dumping, the parasite eggs will be abandoned by the hen when their adopted siblings hatch. Parasitic species make up for this lowered survival rate by laying many more eggs.

Surprisingly, nest parasitism does not seem to diminish the chances of survival for the host ducklings once they're hatched. Surveys of common goldeneyes, which are occasionally parasitized by hooded mergansers, have shown that about as many goldeneyes survive to fledging in nests that have been invaded as in nests that haven't. This may be because ducklings forage for themselves almost from hatching, and so the adopted siblings aren't directly depriving the host ducklings of food.

Eiders are colonial nesters, and up to 10 000 may breed in one place. Their down-lined nests are often located within a duck length of each other. Such a concentration of passive

protein is a magnet for predators—foxes, skunks, ravens, and gulls. Some of the birds isolate their nests on offshore islands. Others make their nests among those of gulls or terns, which are better able to ward off predators. The cost to this strategy is that as the ducklings hatch, they may fall prey to gulls themselves.

Once incubation begins, ducks will defend their nests with varying degrees of determination. Cavity-nesters are the most protective of their clutches and young—perhaps because escape is usually impractical by the time a nest has been discovered. The goldeneye mother will hiss at intruders from inside her nest.

Many ground-nesters will employ the famous broken-wing gambit to lure predators away from their eggs. When a predator approaches, the mother duck feigns injury by stumbling away from her eggs dragging a half-open wing—hopefully before the nest has been spotted. Most predators find injured prey irresistible, and the mother staggers just beyond the reach of the attacker to lure it from her brood. In general, ducks are less aggressive than geese or swans but will attempt to bite animals threatening their eggs or will beat them with their wings. Once the exact location of the nest is known to a predator, the hen, with her rounded bill and webbed feet, is poorly equipped to defend her eggs. Over half of all duck nests are lost to predators.

The hazards to the hen and her brood are many, but ducks are persistent nesters. If a predator drives a mother duck from the nest and eats her eggs, chances are she will nest again—which means that she will have to repeat the rituals of courtship, mating, and nest building. In the higher latitudes, where summers are short, some ducks won't

LEFT: *As with many duck species, population numbers for the northern pintail reached a 10-year peak in 1997— partly due to flooding through much of the prairie provinces and mid-western states during that year. For 30 years, the northern pintail's numbers have been in decline, while other ducks have thrived. Worldwide, however, it is still one of the most abundant of ducks.*

have time to lay a second clutch, but where summers are long enough, ducks have been known to renest up to three times in a single season.

To keep the eggs warm, the hen plucks feathers from her breast to line the nest and cover the eggs in her absence. The skin she exposes on her breast is called a brood patch, and it transfers much more heat from her body to the eggs than skin covered in feathers. The eggs take from three to five weeks to hatch.

Periodically, the brooding hen turns the eggs with her bill. Throughout incubation, she will leave her clutch once or twice a day in order to feed and bathe. The hooded merganser makes feeding forays as often as four or five times a day, probably because of this species' small size and higher metabolism. Despite the frequency of these absences, the hen will still lose about 15 percent of her body weight while incubating.

As incubation proceeds, most ducks become increasingly reluctant to leave their eggs. Although the females of some species will feed even as the eggs are hatching, most will not leave the nest in the final 48 hours of incubation. As hatching time nears, eider and oldsquaw ducks enter a stage of acquiescence during which researchers taking egg counts can actually lift the mother off the nest and set her back down again with almost no protest. It's an instinctive response to her rising level of investment in the clutch, and the diminishing likelihood of successfully hatching a second brood if anything should happen to this one. Or perhaps she is simply determined to claim the last few hours of peace that she will know before hatching begins, and a storm of peeping down is upon her.

RIGHT: *Guide books sometimes describe the cinnamon teal as a rather plain, brown duck, but this photo shows off the male cinnamon's rich, rusty color. It's difficult for anyone but an expert to distinguish the female from the blue-winged teal hen. Cinnamon teals feed much as northern shovelers do, sieving the water for microscopic organisms, but also taking the seeds and leaves of aquatic plants.*

SHELL TO SKY

BEYOND THE NEST

W hat is whispered from one calcium cell to the next only the duckling knows, but the ideal hatching comes off like a prison break, everyone escaping at once. The sound of the first nestling to peck at its shell, conducted from egg to egg, probably urges its siblings to join in. A soft clucking from the mother may also stimulate the hatching. Within a short time, the nest is crackling with the sounds of ducklings chipping their way out of their shells. The emergent ducklings have a horny bump called an egg tooth on the tip of their upper beak. They use it to help break out of their shells— an exhausting process that may take anywhere from a few hours to a full day. They shed the egg tooth shortly after hatching.

For up to a day, the hatchlings remain covered by their mother as their downy feathers dry and their limbs gain strength. During this time, they imprint upon their

PREVIOUS PAGE, LEFT: *Throughout their life cycle, ducks are culled by predators. On average, less than half of all eggs laid survive to hatch, only half of all ducklings hatched survive to fledging, and slightly more than half of all fledgling birds survive to nest. The death rate among most animals surviving to adulthood drops dramatically, but because the duck's single greatest predator—human hunters—takes adult birds almost exclusively, the duck enjoys no such reprieve.*

PREVIOUS PAGE, RIGHT: *Duck nests suffer very high predation rates. In some areas, as few as 10 percent of all eggs laid ever hatch. Mortality rates are especially high on prairie farmland, where reduced groundcover makes nests easy for predators to find. Fortunately, ducks lay high numbers of eggs compared to other birds and will often mate and nest again if their first or even their second clutch is destroyed.*

mother's voice and appearance. As with all waterfowl, ducklings identify the first large, moving thing they see as their mother and follow her wherever she goes. In this way, they come to identify themselves as ducks of their own species.

The mother's first task is to lead the ducklings to water to begin feeding. This can be a long trip for them if the nest is far from water, but ducklings can walk well almost immediately.

In the case of tree-nesters such as the wood duck, they have to get to the ground first. The first hurdle—literally—is to scale the walls inside their nest to the exit hole. Their webbed feet are clawed from birth, enabling most of them to make this short climb. But once on the brink, they may be faced with a descent of three or four stories to the forest floor or, if they're lucky, the water.

LEFT: *This eider nest is the exclusive charge of the hen, who will lay an egg a day until her clutch is complete (up to a dozen eggs, but more usually four or five). Once incubation begins, she leaves the nest only briefly to feed and bathe, and her mate abandons her. One veteran eider observer did see a male approach an unattended nest, rearrange the eggs with his bill, then settle down on the clutch. Apparently, seven minutes of fatherhood was enough to satisfy the drake's curiosity before he abandoned his adopted family.*

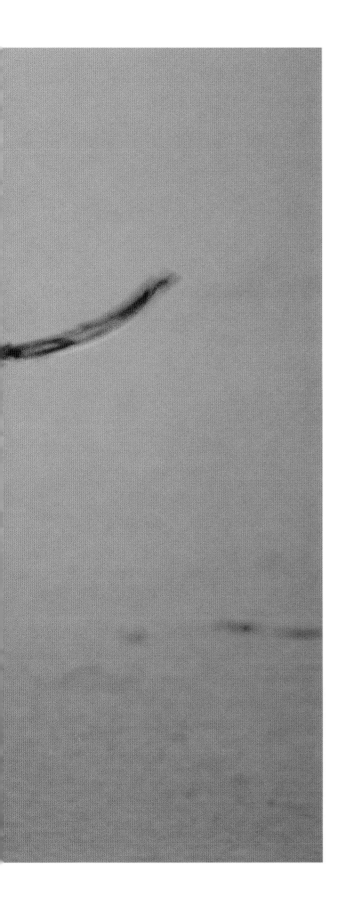

The hens are as incapable of carrying their young as they are of carrying nesting materials. The only help they seem able to provide their offspring is to fly to the base of the tree and call to them. One at a time, the ducklings climb to the nest hole, spread their wings and feet, and make the leap. They can't fly, but their down offers enough air resistance that the young chicks fall quite slowly, and are rarely injured. Their down also cushions their landing.

These are amazing feats when one compares duckling development to that of song-birds, which need weeks of brooding before they can leave their nests. Once down from the tree, there's no going back. Their mother will find a suitable spot close to the water to raise her young.

The mother duck does not assist her young in feeding other than to lead them to food. Young ducks instinctively snap at anything small and dark, either in the water or on the way to it. Through trial and error, they learn what is edible and what is not.

In the Arctic, oldsquaw and eider ducklings eat large quantities of mosquito larvae. Within minutes of entering the water, they are capable of brief dives. Regardless of their adult diet, most ducklings feed on insects, their larvae, and other small aquatic inverte-brates for the first few weeks. A completely vegetable diet cannot provide them with the protein needed for their rapid growth.

Ducklings are more vulnerable to predators than they will be at any later stage of their lives. Ravens, gulls, and birds of prey swoop down on them from the air. On the water, bullfrogs, bass, pike, and snapping turtles pull them under, never to surface again. Marine ducks are eaten by seals, salmon, sharks, and gulls—almost anything for which a duckling is a mouthful. Most hens confine their broods to smaller bodies of fresh water for the first few weeks.

The mountain streams where the harlequin raises its young conceal few predators, but the water itself is dangerous to ducklings, which have yet to learn how to shoot the rapids. Until they do, the mother harlequin steers her brood to the quieter pools and back eddies.

Ducklings are not entirely defenseless. When threatened from above, they crash-dive in the blink of an eye. Once underwater, a brood will scatter and emerge in a looser formation. Ordinarily, their top swimming speed is about half a metre (20 inches) per second. But under threat, ducklings switch from their normal paddling to a rapid, plunging movement of their webbed feet, allowing them to hydroplane over the surface as fast as two metres (6 $\frac{1}{2}$ feet) per second.

Their best protection, though, is the warning calls of their mother, which they heed either by following her, or hiding in thick vegetation and staying motionless. No one is quite sure how they know which action to take, but the mother must give them some vocal cue. The duckling's ears are ideally positioned to hear its mother's calls—just below and behind its eyes. With its face in the water, its eyes are submerged, allowing it to search for food, but its ears remain above the surface, within earshot of its mother's warning call.

The mother will also use the broken-wing display to decoy aquatic predators from her brood. Somehow, the ducklings know to hide and remain still.

The mother duck also protects her brood from the elements, covering the growing duck-lings with her wings in cold and rain. Despite her efforts, the duckling queue trailing the hen shrinks during the six to eight weeks between hatching and first flight. Some are taken by

predators and some die of exposure, but on average half of all ducks die within two weeks of hatching.

The surviving ducklings grow rapidly. Within a few days of hatching, juvenile down begins to replace their fuzzy natal down. Within two or three weeks, it covers their bodies in a uniform coat that looks more like plush than feathers. Until contour feathers begin to grow in, the ducklings huddle beneath their mother for warmth. By five to six weeks, contour feathers will have replaced the down and, with the exception of their stubby wings, the juvenile ducks look much like their mothers.

The birds soon begin to practice the skills they will need to survive as adults. Even ducks raised in captivity, separated from their mothers at hatching, seem to develop a full repertoire of natural behaviors. They feed, preen, bathe, fly, and display normally, suggesting these abilities are innate. Nonetheless, these skills need exercising before they can be perfected.

Diving is essential for ducks that feed underwater. Ducklings are even more buoyant than their parents, and analysis of high-speed films has shown that juveniles dive by jumping from the surface of the water and plunging in headfirst before kicking their way down. Using this technique, mergansers can chase small fish within their first few days on the water. Each day, the ducklings need a full eight hours of feeding on the water to satisfy their ravenous appetites.

The wings and flight feathers are the last parts of the duck's body to develop. While primary flight feathers grow, the shafts are filled with blood to supply them with the nutrients they need. When they reach their full size, the blood drains from the shaft and they become rooted to the bones. During this time, the young birds exercise their wing muscles for their first flights with static tests—flapping their wings without actually taking off.

Often, a duck's initial attempts at flying are from the water, and begin with long taxis over the surface. Learning to fly over water has the advantages of clear runways and a yielding surface on which to land. At six to eight weeks after hatching, a duck's first successful flight—usually a turn around the pond or marsh—is often accompanied by much calling from its siblings, which seem almost to cheer it on.

Simultaneously, the duck undergoes behavioral changes. It starts to lose its aversion for ducks outside its immediate family. It takes flight with other juveniles and loses contact with its siblings. Ironically, as her brood fledges, the hen enters her molt and loses her own ability to fly. But by then, there is nothing more she can do to help them. When her flight feathers have grown in again and she rejoins the autumn staging, her young—though she may find them—will be part of the surging flock.

LEFT: *These mallard ducklings are still sporting their natal down. Down feathers make excellent insulation but do not function as air foils. Before they can fly, their down will have to be replaced by flight feathers, which won't grow in for several more weeks. In the meantime, the chicks huddle together for warmth.*

PREVIOUS PAGE: *Ducks and other waterfowl are incapable of using their bills to carry objects any distance—either nesting material or their own young. Unfortunately for this duckling, herons do not share this inability. Herons wait motionless, with their beaks poised like forceps, to pluck fish or amphibians from the water. But like most predators, they are opportunists, and a young duck will do very nicely.*

ABOVE: *Many ducklings have eye-stripes—a line of dark plumage running through the eye. This not only camouflages the young duckling by breaking up the outline of its head, but may also prevent its siblings, which instinctively peck at anything small and dark as they learn to forage, from poking it in the eye.*

RIGHT: *One study showed that ducklings swimming in their mother's wake expend only 47 percent of the energy expended by ducklings swimming on their own. The last duck in the line swims with the least effort, but is also the most likely to be eaten by predators, which often attack from the rear.*

ON AUTUMN'S STAGE

THE PASSAGE OF DUCKS

As the days grow shorter, the young birds congregate in longer test flights. The older ducks that have recovered from their molts join them in the marshes and the process of staging—flock formation for the autumn migration—begins. The birds travel farther and higher on their foraging flights until one day, when an approaching front brings favorable winds, they begin the journey south.

In North America, most ducks fly down large river valleys and between the major mountain chains on routes known as flyways. The four main north-south flyways in North America are the Pacific, Central, Mississippi, and Atlantic. In peak years, some 100 million ducks travel these aerial corridors.

The search for a milder climate in which to winter doesn't always mean migrating south. The king eider, which breeds in the high Arctic, migrates more in longitude than

PREVIOUS PAGE, LEFT: *While migration is obviously a huge expenditure of energy for waterfowl, it also offers them many benefits: They can feed off the summer abundance of the tundra without having to endure the hardships of winter in the far north. By feeding on the move, they can exploit local abundances and move on before predators can gather to hunt, and finally they can sequester themselves in large or isolated wetlands during their flightless molts.*

PREVIOUS PAGE, RIGHT: *The spectacled eider is so named for obvious reasons. These are birds of the high Arctic. Their range is so remote that, until recently, no one knew where they wintered. Then, in the spring of 1995, studies using transponders attached to the birds revealed that they migrate from Alaska's North Slope to openings in the sea ice of the Bering Sea, where they are able to feed on marine shellfish.*

latitude in its flight to wintering areas on the Bering Sea or North Atlantic. Many cavity-nesting ducks move from inland forests and bogs to open water on the coast.

One northern duck is so well adapted to the cold that it has no interest in a more hospitable climate. Until 1995, no one knew where most spectacled eider ducks went in winter; they just seemed to disappear from their breeding grounds on Alaska's North Slope. Biologists from the U.S. Fish and Wildlife Service had attached radio transmitters to some two dozen nesting spectacled eiders in the hope of tracking them to their wintering grounds. The plan foundered when the eiders' high body temperature kept the transmitters' batteries too warm and they all failed after only a few months.

LEFT: *The fulvous whistling duck is found on four continents: North and South America, Africa and Asia. Curiously, there seems to be no difference between individuals from these completely isolated populations. This duck is gregarious, and the males share in the incubation and rearing of the young.*

Six months later, one transmitter suddenly began broadcasting again just as the biologists were about to begin an aerial search. Thanks to the Lazarus-like revival of that one beacon, the biologists found the ducks almost 200 kilometres (120 miles) off Alaska's west coast, in the middle of the Bering Sea. An estimated 150 000 ducks were filling any break in the sea ice. Apparently, these patches of open water are the only windows to the rich invertebrate life below, the eiders' principal food.

Just how ducks migrate is still something of a mystery. It has been proven that many birds have the ability to fly in a constant compass direction. But to navigate, a bird or other animal must know not only its direction of travel, but its starting location and destination. The most popular theory holds that birds gauge their global position by observing the arc of the sun or stars for even a short period of time. Human navigators do the same with instruments. By knowing the time and estimating the position of the sun at its highest point, we can determine both latitude and longitude, and so our place on the global grid. For the ducks, we can only assume these calculations are made on some instinctive level. When flying to a place they've been before, they probably zero in on their final destination by watching for familiar landmarks. Under cloudy skies, they may rely on landmarks to keep them on track until they can get another look at the sun. But none of this quite explains how a pintail can take off from a pond on a cloudy morning and continue its migration in the right direction.

Whatever method the ducks use, it's highly reliable. The females consistently return to the place of their hatching, and the males follow the females.

Most of the dabbling and perching ducks migrate at much higher altitudes than they normally fly—somewhere between 300 and 900 metres (1000 and 3000 feet). Flocks have been found flying as high as 6100 metres (20 000 feet). Marine species tend to fly low over water, with their wings almost touching the waves on the downstroke.

Many ducks fly as fast as 80 kilometres (50 miles) an hour—the canvasback has been clocked at over 112 kilometres (70 miles) per hour—but they must rest more often than other migratory birds. Because they have large bodies in relation to their wings, they do not glide well. Just to maintain altitude, ducks must beat their wings rapidly—some at almost 300 strokes per minute in level flight. Consequently, flying is an extremely energetic process for a duck.

Flying in formation may conserve some of that energy. The assumption is that each bird flying in a V or echelon (half a V) should be able to gain lift from the upwash trailing the nearest wing of the bird in front of it. In theory, if the birds in a formation held their positions perfectly, they could fly with half the effort of flying solo. Analysis of motion picture footage of Canada geese in flight has led some scientists to conclude that, in practice, the geese are probably experiencing energy savings closer to 8 or 10 percent. The smaller a bird is, the more exactly it must hold its position to save energy through formation flying—which is probably why we don't see chickadees flying in Vs.

An alternative theory is that ducks and geese don't save any appreciable energy by flying in a V, but adopt the formation because flying behind and to one side of another bird is the best position for keeping it in sight. In doing so, they may be continually checking one another's direction of flight—in effect, navigating by consensus.

Migrating ducks begin their day by taking flight before dawn. By late morning, they begin to search for open water where they can feed and rest. Ducks able to feed on grains will also land in farmers' fields, preferably ones bordered by water.

It is at these times that ducks are most vulnerable to their greatest natural enemies, the birds of prey. Raptors usually surprise their prey from above, diving straight onto their quarry or leveling off at the last second and swooping into them. But surprising a duck isn't all that easy. A duck's eyes are on the sides of its head. The field of view of each duck eye overlaps that of its other eye slightly, giving the duck 360-degree vision. Its only blind spot is below, so it's difficult for a bird of prey to dive on a lone duck without being spotted, let alone a flock with hundreds of pairs of eyes.

On the water, ducks dive to avoid raptors, usually changing direction several times before surfacing. The scattering of a flock in air or on water also confuses predators. If a duck in flight spots a falcon, it will drop into high groundcover such as cattails or grass. A dabbling duck can take off surrounded by groundcover but falcons and eagles need a clear approach to become airborne, so they are usually reluctant to follow the duck down.

In a successful stoop, the predator delivers the initial blow with balled talons, then finishes the job on the ground by piercing the duck's spine or lungs. Despite the popular image, raptors rarely snatch their prey in midair.

On average, ducks evade two out of three attacks by falcons or eagles. Some biologists estimate that falcons feeding on waterfowl kill up to two birds a day. This is far more than they can eat, but because only a large falcon or an eagle can actually carry off an adult duck, other predators—including coyotes, otters, cats, foxes, or raptors—often steal their kills before they can finish them.

These scavengers also kill ducks themselves. Surprisingly, a study by the National Biological Survey in the United States showed that in the prairie pothole region, where most of North America's ducks nest, fewer kills occurred in areas frequented by coyotes. Biologists believe that coyotes may drive out foxes, which are probably the major mammalian predator of both adult ducks and their eggs.

The combination of these hazards is harrowing, and life for the average duck is brief. Although a big duck like the king eider can live 15 years, smaller ducks seldom live more than three. Six is a ripe old age for a mallard. But ducks face even worse hazards than their natural enemies.

For ducks traveling the four great flyways, human hunters are the greatest danger. Each year, hunters kill an estimated 20 million migrating ducks—about the same number as are killed by all other predators combined. Their only defense against the shotgun is the calendar, as most states and provinces now enforce fairly strict seasonal regulations and bag limits.

Hunters continue to kill ducks long after the smell of cordite has left the air. Millions of dabbling ducks swallow lead shot lying at the bottoms of ponds and marshes in areas where hunters have been active for the past century. Most will survive the ingestion of a single pellet, but rarely two or three. Lead poisoning impairs coordination and the ducks usually die staggering about on land, unable even to lift their wings. Raptors and

LEFT: *The flock offers the same protections to ducks that it affords all birds: the improved surveillance of many eyes, and the confounding effect of many bodies. On the water, most ducks instinctively dive when threatened by flying or swimming predators. Ducks change direction several times while swimming underwater, making it difficult for a predator to predict where the duck will surface.*

PREVIOUS PAGE: *Duck hunting was so popular during the reigns of the later Egyptian Pharaohs that it became necessary to issue "marsh tickets" — probably the world's first hunting licenses. One ancient scribe advised, "Love writing, shun dancing; then you become a worthy official. Do not long for the marsh ticket. Turn your back on the throw stick and chase."*

other predators feeding regularly on the poisoned ducks accumulate lead in their bodies and eventually suffer the same fate.

Fortunately, lead shot has been banned in the United States since the fall of 1991, and replaced largely by steel. Canada followed with similar legislation in the fall of 1996 and both countries have since outlawed lead fishing sinkers. Hunters objected to the bans because steel shot is less effective at bringing down game and causes more wear on gun barrels. Unfortunately, with over 260 pellets discharged from a single shotgun shell, there are still billions of them lying in the bottoms of prairie sloughs. It's estimated that currently 2 to 3 percent of the fall duck migration is fatally poisoned each year. Many more survive for years with pellets embedded in their flesh, but at least those will now be made of steel, which is much less toxic.

Ducks are considerably more resistant to metal poisoning than many other animals. Feathers are made of keratin, a protein consisting largely of sulfur-based amino acids. Metals in the bloodstream will replace the sulfur atom in these amino acids. When the duck molts, it sheds not only its feathers, but the metals contained in the keratin. With two annual molts, ducks are especially good at ridding their bodies of lead in this way.

Lead is less of a problem than the tonnes of pesticides and herbicides we spray on our crops and open fields every year. Eventually, these chemicals all end up in the water. The prairie pothole region is a band of shallow ponds about 500 kilometres (300 miles) wide and 1600 kilometres (1000 miles) long, sprawled across the geographic center of North America. The region is relatively arid, but because of poor soil drainage, spring runoff turns the millions of depressions gouged out by glaciers during the last ice age into shallow ponds.

LEFT: *The American black duck is one of the few dabbling ducks in which the male and female cannot be distinguished at a glance. Both look quite similar to a dark female mallard—a species that the black duck also resembles in feeding habits, courtship, and voice.*

Warmed by the summer sun, the potholes are amazingly productive, home to a buffet of aquatic plants, microbes, insect larvae, snails, fish, and frogs. Although the pothole region constitutes only 10 percent of North America's duck breeding grounds, over half the continent's ducks are hatched there every year. It's a virtual duck factory.

The potholes collect not just life, but agricultural runoff as well. As the summer progresses and water evaporates from the ponds, the pesticides and herbicides in them are concentrated. The threat they pose to ducks is not so much direct poisoning as starvation. The toxins kill the plants and insects living in the ponds, leaving less and less for the ducks to eat as the summer wears on. As the smaller potholes dry up, the ducks crowd into the remaining sloughs and ponds, leaving them more vulnerable to predators and disease.

To many farmers, the potholes are simply a nuisance they have to steer a combine or a plow around and a waste of land that could be producing crops. While some farmers go out of their way to avoid a nesting site, others are inclined to plow and harvest as close to the margins of the potholes as they can, destroying many nests and leaving little cover for those that do escape the blade. The survival rate for nests on farmland is as low as 10 percent in many areas, compared to about 50 percent for all duck species in North America. In the pothole region of North Dakota alone, over 900 000 adult hens are killed annually by mammalian predators such as raccoons, foxes, and skunks.

The prairies are not the only place where ducks must compete for shrinking resources. Although 90 percent of the original wetlands of California's Central Valley has been lost to agriculture and housing, the region still attracts some 12 million wintering waterfowl

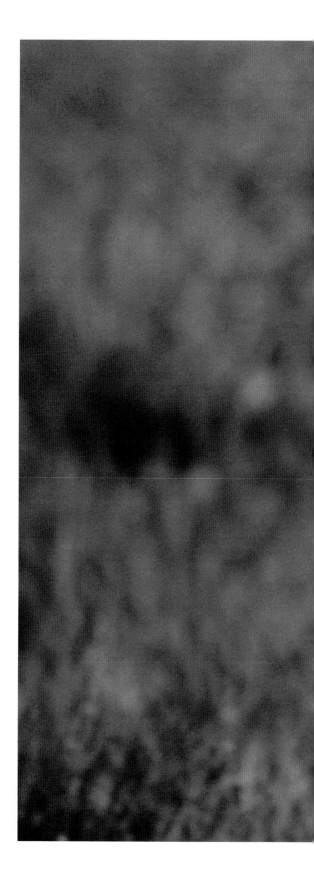

annually. In 1972, the U.S. Bureau of Reclamation completed a 132-kilometre (82-mile) concrete canal to carry agricultural runoff water to a series of evaporation ponds covering some 520 hectares (1300 acres) adjacent to the existing San Luis Wildlife Refuge. Originally, the ponds were to be drained into the valley's river system, but that phase of construction was never completed.

Tens of thousands of wintering waterfowl flocked to the ponds and the surrounding marshes, which were designated the Kesterson National Wildlife Refuge. The project seemed a success both for the farmers and the waterfowl. But by 1983, managers at the Kesterson Refuge began to observe deaths among adult birds and deformities of hatchlings, including missing eyes and malformed legs, wings, and bills. Sampling revealed that as the runoff water evaporated, minerals and salts were concentrated in the marsh—in particular, selenium, a naturally occurring element that is vital for most animals' health in trace amounts, but toxic at higher levels.

Until they could flush the reserve with fresh water, Bureau of Reclamation workers had to frighten away waterfowl with fireworks and other noisemakers. Fish and Wildlife biologists warned that just flushing the wetlands would not remove the selenium, which was by then chemically bound up in the plant matter and sediment of the marshes. They were right. The flushing plan failed and the flow of drain water to Kesterson was cut off in 1986. It is now diverted directly to the San Joaquin River, which carries it to the sea. The original Kesterson reservoir and the surrounding wetlands still support up to 100 000 overwintering waterfowl, but the evaporation ponds are now under half a metre (two feet) of clean fill. The Bureau of Reclamation literally had to bury its mistake.

LEFT: *Experiments to discover how migratory birds navigate have been confounded by contradictory results. The most popular theory is that they are somehow able to quickly determine both their compass direction as well as their global position by relatively cursory observation of the sun. Some ducks are successfully able to navigate over migrations up to 6100 kilometres (3800 miles).*

PREVIOUS PAGE: *With their green heads, male northern shovelers resemble mallards at first glance, but are distinguished by their proportionately larger bills. Northern shovelers have been nicknamed "neighbor's mallards" by some hunters. Because of the inferior taste of the shoveler's flesh, it's more likely to be given away.*

Thankfully, other stories in the history of duck conservation have happier endings. The wood duck, perhaps the most beautiful of North America's waterfowl, may also have once been our most abundant duck. The male's plumage, striking for its rich colors and sharp delineation, seems to have caught the attention of almost every American naturalist who ever picked up a pen. They kept giving it new names: Carolina duck, tree duck, bride duck, acorn duck.

It was also known for the delicacy of its flesh, and hunters in the 19th century shot it without bag or season limits. Commercial hunters caught up to 600 in a single day. In a few cases, special "punt guns," with bores of up to 5 centimetres (2 inches) were mounted on the decks of barges much like a modern whaler's harpoon gun. The punts were poled out to rafts of waterfowl, which were then much tamer. As many as a hundred birds would be killed with a single blast. They were sold by the thousands in public markets.

At the same time, the bottomland forests where the wood duck lives and breeds were being cut at a record rate. By the turn of the century, some naturalists were warning of the wood duck's imminent extinction. These warnings were probably premature. There have always been healthy populations in the forests of British Columbia and Washington and the bayous of the southern United States, but hunters were alarmed by the decline in local populations.

Louisiana banned the hunting of wood ducks completely in 1904, and 20 other states soon followed suit. In 1916, they were protected under the Migratory Bird Treaty

LEFT: *Barrow's goldeneye has an unusual distribution and migration pattern. In North America, the main population nests in tree cavities and sometimes rock crevices in a wide band following the coast from the Aleutians down to California. A second, small population breeds in Labrador. Both winter in salt water. Whether these widely separated populations were once part of a larger, contiguous distribution, or whether one was seeded by a stray pair, we can only guess.*

RIGHT: *Early in this century, wood duck populations were decimated by hunters and habitat destruction throughout much of its range in the eastern United States. Clubs of dedicated hunters and conservationists mounted a massive campaign of nest box building to compensate for the loss of the wood duck's natural nesting cavities—mainly holes in old trees. The ducks took readily to the artificial nests, and under strict hunting bans imposed by many states their numbers rebounded. Today, there are probably over 100 000 such boxes in North America.*

with Canada. Under the ban, the wood duck's numbers began to recover. The ban lasted until 1941, when a limit of one duck a day was allowed.

At about the same time that the complete hunting ban was lifted, private clubs and government agencies began building nesting boxes by the thousands to offset the loss of natural nesting cavities. The wood duck hen lays large clutches of eggs, up to 16 in a single brood, and if her nest is destroyed, like most ducks she is capable of renesting up to twice in the same season. The wood ducks took to the artificial nests willingly and today—thanks to their fecundity and the efforts of conservationists—they again number in the millions.

The irony is that hunters have become the duck's greatest allies. As with so many animals, the main threat to duck populations is not the individuals taken by hunters, but the destruction of habitat. In North America, some 70 to 80 percent of the original wetlands have been drained and filled since the arrival of European settlers. Forests, which are as vital to cavity-nesting ducks as marshes are to the dabblers, have fared almost as poorly. Recognizing the importance of habitat conservation, hunters have organized themselves into powerful lobbying and conservation groups. Since its inception in 1937, Ducks Unlimited alone has protected over 6.5 million hectares (16 million acres) of wetlands in North America. This habitat has benefited hundreds of marsh and aquatic species, including ducks. Although few duck populations are anywhere near historic levels, most species have either held their own or increased in the last 15 years.

Duck species have adapted with varying success to agriculture and urbanization. The harlequin demands such pristine habitat that human activity as benign as kayaking may evict it

from some mountain rivers. At the other extreme, the mallard seems able to nest near almost any body of water bigger than a swimming pool as long as a few tall weeds grow nearby.

Every spring, local news stations air footage of a mallard hen leading her brood through traffic or dabbling in some public fountain. In our homes, we imprint the familiar rune of migration on everything from sleeping bags to wallpaper. But all of the upholstery we pattern with the coming and going of the duck cannot keep us from looking up at the rushing of wings.

Even from the glass canyons of our cities, the vane of autumn draws our gaze skyward. As the duck abandons us to shorter days and longer shadows, who does not yearn after the compass of the flock, or rejoice in the promise of its return?

LEFT: *The canvasback is a favorite among hunters, in part because of its weight. As the largest of the freshwater diving ducks, one might think the canvasback an easy target, but it compensates for its size with a wariness of human beings and a top flight speed of 110 kilometres (70 miles) per hour.*

ABOVE: *On the wings of many ducks is a patch of color called the speculum, or wing window. The speculum often appears on both sexes and is made of particularly colorful secondary flight feathers. The speculum may serve as a signal to other ducks in flight that helps keep the flock together. It is also prominent in many courtship displays.*

RIGHT: *Like most diving ducks, the common merganser needs a good stretch of open water in which to taxi before becoming airborne. Unlike its relative, the red-breasted merganser, the common merganser does most of its foraging in freshwater lakes and ponds.*

SUGGESTED READING

Driver, Peter M. *In Search of the Eider.* London: The Saturn Press, Ltd., 1974.

Furtman, Michael. *On the Wings of the North Wind.* Harrisburg, Pennsylvania: Stackpole Books, 1991.

Gooders, John and Trevor Boyer. *Ducks of Canada and the Northern Hemisphere.* New York: Dragon's World Ltd., 1986.

Johnsgard, Paul A. *A Guide to North American Waterfowl.* Bloomington: Indiana University Press, 1979.

Lack, David. *Evolution Illustrated by Waterfowl.* Oxford: Blackwell Scientific Publications, 1974.

Nielsen, Scott. *Mallards.* Stillwater, Minnesota: Voyageur Press, Inc., 1992.

Phillips, John C. *A Natural History of the Ducks.* New York: Dover Publications, Inc., 1922.

Shurtleff, Lawton L. and Christopher Savage. *The Wood Duck and the Mandarin.* Berkeley: University of California Press, 1996.

Todd, Frank S. *Waterfowl: Ducks, Geese and Swans of the World.* San Diego: Sea World Press, 1979.

Todd, Frank S. *Natural History of the Waterfowl.* Vista, California: Ibis Publishing, 1996.

INTERNET SITES

Duckdata home page: http://www.nwrc.nbs.gov/duckdata/duckdata.html
Ducks Unlimited: http://www.ducks.org
U.S. Fish and Wildlife Service, Office of Migratory Bird Management:
http://www.fws.gov/r9mbmo/

INDEX

Bold entries refer to photographs.

PHOTO CREDITS

Ferdinand Mels / First Light vi–vii

Aubrey Lang x, 36, 47

Wayne Lynch 1, 6, 9, 11, 19, 22, 24, 41, 43, 50, 51, 56, 67, 68, 78, 79, 81, 82, 105

Victoria Hurst 2, 77, 84, 87

Thomas Kitchin 5, 14, 15, 16, 17, 20–21, 26, 29, 30, 33, 34, 48, 55, 58, 66, 80, 88, 95, 96, 99, 102

Thomas Kitchin / First Light 12, 40

Jerry Kobalenko / First Light 18

Tim Christie 23, 42, 44, 64, 91, 101

Robert Lankinen / First Light 38, 61, 92

Terry Attard 39, 63, 74, 104

Peter McLeod / First Light 53

Victoria Hurst / First Light 70

Julie Habel / First Light 73